The Venetian Ghetto

Text by Anna-Vera Sullam and Riccardo Calimani
Photographs by Davide Calimani

Electa

*The square
of Ghetto Novo:.
to the left, one
of the Monuments
to the Holocaust.*

Contents

*The square
of the Ghetto Novo:
in the background,
one of the
Monuments
to the Holocaust,
to the right, the
Nursing Home.*

*Opposite page:
Guglie Bridge,
the canals
and foundations
of Cannareggio
where one of the
Ghetto Vecchio's
entrances can
be found.*

*Pages 4 and 5:
the square
of the Ghetto Novo:
to the left, the
portico and façade
of the Italian
Schola.*

*Pages 6 and 7:
the snow-covered
square of Ghetto
Novo with the
German Schola
to the left and
the Italian Schola
to the right.*

*Pages 8 and 9:
the square
of Ghetto Novo
and the bridge
leading to the
Ghetto Vecchio
in high-water.*

*Pages 10 and 11:
the Israeli
Nursing Home
and square
of the Ghetto Novo.*

The Venetian Ghetto: a centennial history

From the first beginnings to the creation of the ghetto

When did the first Jews arrive to the islands emerging from the lagoon?

Proof of antique Jewish existence can be found in the use of the name Giudecca. In the 18th century, Ludovico Muratori wrote in his *Dissertazione* that in 1090 the name Giudecca was already in circulation and that this went to prove the presence of Jews on the island, whereas Thomas Temanza discovered an antique map, drawn during the 16th century by a Franciscan, upon which the island of Spinalunga is depicted with the name of *Judaica*. Others sustain that certain families, having been accused of conspiracy against the Republic and sent in exile to the island of Spinalunga, was proof enough that the term derived from "del giudicato" ("judged") and that this in Venetian dialect was then transformed into "Zudegà" and further on "Judecha," "Zuecca" and finally "Giudaica."

The question, nevertheless, remains unanswered as over and above the opinion of historians, no concrete proof of Jewish presence on the island can be traced prior to the 14th century. Among the copious 14th-century documentation that testifies to the presence or passing through of Jews in the lagoon territory, one in particular is the Decree of 1386, with which the Venetian Senate granted the Jews an isolated area of the Lido for the burying of their loved ones. Whilst the year prior, in 1385, an agreement was stipulated between the Senate and certain Jewish lenders in Mestre for the granting of loans to the poorer people of the city.

With this agreement the Venetian State was able to reduce the internal political tension that had emerged by controlling the poverty and directing, at the same time, the hostility of the population towards the Jewish usurers, who would soon become the scapegoats of the political powers not only in Venice. The agreement between Venice and the Jews, named "Condotta" ("Conduct") was full of detailed codicils and regulations born out of a laborious attention to detail. The formal outline was more or less constant. The following were stipulated: the conditions and type of loans, the number of banks able to grant said loans, the location of these banks and their hours of trade. The Jews were offered permits to stay but they had to guarantee low interest rates on loans and to act within the powers of the political oligarchy in force in Venice at the time, which imposed higher taxes on the Jews. The Jews had the privilege, however, of being able to autonomously elect their leaders, who were then given the responsibility of fixing the individual share of the "burden." Their role as lenders was confirmed definitively in the 15th century. Excluded from the arts and master skills, from public office and the military forces, from free-lance professionalism and the possibility of owning land, the Jews were left with their only chance of survival: the money market, prohibited from Christian religion.

In 1508, with the eruption of war against the League of Cambrai, Venice was quickly robbed of the entire hinterland of the city and enemy troops advanced at an alarming rate. Many refugees, among them numerous Jews, took shelter in the lagoon. Even the Jewish bankers from Mestre took refuge in the city, who were able to travel between the lagoon and the mainland but were not permitted to reside in the lagoon city for more than fifteen days at a time. They were welcomed, how-

ever, seeing as they had brought their capital with them, a very well-received commodity in such a delicate time. Following the defeat of Agnadello in 1509 the situation became more dramatic: bands of French, Spanish and Imperial troops arrived to threaten the city, landing on the banks of the lagoon. This sequence of negative events left indelible signs on the soul of the citizens and the Venetian nobility. A gloomy state of mind followed; the Franciscan preachers repeatedly exclaimed that what was needed was a re-conquering of the favour of God and for each person to repent for their sins in order for the Republic to survive. One of the most serious of sins, however, was to freely allow Jews to live within the lagoon city.

On 20 March 1516, when danger was almost over, Zaccaria Dolfin, in the Collegio, harshly attacked the Jews, accusing them of illegally building synagogues and corrupting the State. He requested that they be confined to the Ghetto Novo (New Ghetto), antique location similar to a fortress in the parish of San Gerolamo. The Doge approved of this request along with certain other patrons and on 29 March a decree was issued that recited: "All Jews are to live together in the courtyard houses that are found in the ghetto within the parish of San Gerolamo; and to prevent that they do not roam around at night: at the edge of the Ghetto Vecchio (Old Ghetto) and the Ghetto Novo two small access bridges will be utilised, to be found on either side of these locations, that will be fitted with gates that will be opened in the morning when the

A Jew,
illustration from
G. Grevembroch,
Gli habiti de'
Veneziani, *18th
century,* Venice,
Museo Correr.

Marangona peals and locked at midnight. Four Christian custodians, who are to be government deputies and paid by same Jews at a price fixed by us, will watch these gates." The ghetto's enclosure was to be completed with two high walls: all exits were to be closed and the doors and windows that faced onto the external part of the ghetto were to be walled in. The custodians were assigned the task of surveying the gates both day and night: the Jews had to pay for two boats that were constantly travelled up and down the canals in the surrounding area. Any Jew found outside the ghetto at nighttime faced a very heavy punishment: a fine for the first and second offences, a heavier fine and two months imprisonment for the third.

In past centuries, a foundry was present in the area, called *getto* in Venetian dialect (from the Italian *gettare* or *fondere* (meaning to cast, merge etc.). Giuseppe Tassini in his publication *Curiosità Veneziana* wrote that this area "ideo vocabatur el getto quia erant ibi ultra duodecim fornaces." Among the contemporary historians, Benjamin Ravid noted that in original documentation relative to the constitution of the ghetto the words *geto* and *getto* were utilised and, from 1541, these were substituted with *ghetto* and *gheto*. Other illustrious scholars of this era have formulated a hypothesis that "ghetto" derives from the Jewish *ghet* ("repudiation," "divorce") or that its origins can be found in the Provencal *gaita* ("guard"), given the four guards who watched the enclosed area. Some Jews coming from Provence would have easily been able to introduce the term to Venice. However, prior to putting forward this hypothesis, it is important to note, nevertheless, that the major part of the scholars favour the Venetian origin of the name. The Jews, however, present in Venice and other similar localities that were subsequently founded in various Italian cities, called their ghetto *chatzer* ("enclosure" or "fence") and, in Venetian, *hasser*.

From the time that the Jews were enclosed in the ghetto, the possibility of them remaining in the city had to be negotiated each five years. This was achieved via the offering of loans and donations to the Government of the Venetian Republic who, in turn, in 1537, granted the Jews, for the first time, a period of permanence lasting ten years. This agreement was an important turning point for the Venetian Jews who, even though enclosed within the walls of the ghetto, saw their permanence in the city legally recognised. However, it was a precarious permanence, full of tension but with respect to the situation of other Italian and European Jews, was considered positive. So much so that the fame of the Venetian ghetto diffused to the most remote communities of the diaspora.

Following the expulsion of the Jews from Spain (1492) and Portugal (1496), of the many travellers who made their way to Venice the following formed part: vagrant Jews, Marans (converted Jews on pressure from the Iberian Peninsula, however certain Jewish customs were secretly retained) and persons of dubious religion. A veritable bazaar of different nations and civilizations. These Jewish merchants, both the Portuguese and Spanish, were called *Levantini* ("Levantines") due to the fact that prior to arriving in Venice they has passed through certain cities of the East (Salonika and Constantinople). The Most Serene Republic of Venice wasted no time in acknowl-

edging the power of the Levantine Jews and when they lamented the difficult conditions within which they lived in the Ghetto Novo, due to lack of living and storage space, they were granted a long calle and smaller surrounding calle on 2 June 1541 in the vicinity: the Ghetto Vecchio. By night they were still to be enclosed as were the other inhabitants of the ghetto and they were restrained from any non-merchant activity. Meanwhile, the long running contention between the Most Serene Republic of Venice and the Sublime Porte (the government of the Ottoman Empire), transformed into an open battle. During the 1560s, Cyprus was always the target of the wrath of the Turks and Venice offered protection to this island by building more robust defences and sending guards there to watch the area.

At the beginning of July 1570, nevertheless, the fleet of the Ottoman Empire disembarked at Cyprus and following a heroic but futile battle, the entire island fell into Turkish control. Faced with threat of an Ottoman colonisation in the Mediterranean, the Christians put aside all thoughts of uncertainty and opportunity and formed a Holy League, of which their fleet affronted and quashed the Ottoman Empire on 7 October at Lepanto. Following the commotion that resulted from this victory, a renewed demonstration of religion was born. So much so that Alvise Grimani joined the movement to expel all Jews suspected of conniving with the enemy as a result of their commercial activities. However, this proposal was shelved and the Jews were able to remain in Venice until February 1573.

Subsequently, the Senate approved the new regulation, differing greatly from the preceding one, the effects of which would have remained in force until at least the first half of the 17th century. Collection taxes were lowered from 10 percent to 5 percent. The autonomy of the banks was once again reduced. The old-style lending banks, intended as independent productive enterprises, were completely transformed: in their place benefit institutions were founded that were sustained by non-recoverable grants. These were forced upon the Jewish Community and destined to the poorer Christians of the city. Security loans were no longer advantageous but more and more a form of usury.

Notwithstanding the people were willing to live by one's wits and scrape together enough money to get by, the lagoon city suffered greatly: the war had dried up the Republic's funds, political disputes increased, the nobility tended to refuse sea trade, now a more risky undertaking due to the increase in pirating. The lifeblood of Mediterranean commercial activity was once again formed by the fugitives from the Iberian Peninsula and the south of Italy, directed towards all ports, both great and small, in the Mediterranean. Having strong, numerous and far-reaching family ties, contemptible methods, skills in merchant negotiations of any type or order and being polyglots, these new Christians of the Maran stock, returning often to Venice, restored Judaism to the city and revealed their hidden and considered offensive Jewish identity. In June 1579, Daniele Rodriga, a Jewish merchant of Maran origin who had assisted in the opening of a Venetian port at Split, requested authorisation from the Senate to bring to Venice fifty families of Jewish merchants who were willing to pay a levy of one hundred ducats. The Cinque Savi approved

Daniele Rodriga's proposal only much later in 1589, granting these merchants the right to live within the city in total safety, along with their respective families. They were also promised religious freedom and immunity from their past. This grant was limited to a duration of ten years. The merchants were obliged to wear the traditional yellow skull-cap as was their custom. No mention was made of Spanish or Maran Jews or the new Christians but a more soft term of "Ponentine Jews" was used. Following the settlement of the "German Nationals" and the "Levantine Nationals" and the acknowledgement of the "Ponentine Nationals," the three settlements were completed. Together they gave life to the Jewish University, as was called the Jewish community of Venice at the time.

The ghetto

Isolated, marginal, central to the city itself, the ghetto was the Jewish quarter, the theatre of Jewish events of the time. In the Ghetto Novo, residence of banking institutions (red, green and yellow), entry was obtained via the long porticoes underneath the imposingly tall houses—up to as many as nine floors, as can be testified in certain land registries of the 18th century. The square opened out into a circular clearing with all the houses' windows facing this unique focal point. This can still be seen today but on one side, instead of the houses that dominated during this period, the 18th century Israeli Nursing Home can be found: one part of this scene and, in particular, that facing Rio San Gerolamo, is no longer evident. On one side the square leads to the Ghetto Vecchio, a long calle intersected by smaller, twisting calle named "Storta" ("Crooked," "Twisted"), Moresco Court, Orto Court, Calle Barucchi, Campiello delle Scole, Scale Matte. From the other side, connected to the square by a narrow bridge, the Ghetto Novissimo (a smaller zone founded in 1633) can be found, with its small, valuable buildings where no shops or synagogues are present. An exclusive quarter for residences for those later arrivals. The tall buildings of then more than likely stood out more than today, as there was very little surrounding construction. There were many gardens, convents and monasteries and roads made of mud and earth. Communal stairs were made of wood as were all the room partitions and structures of the houses, the divisions between ceilings and attics and those between the small lowered ceiling apartments and the communal services. This to prevent overloading. Often, however, fires erupted and all inhabitants ran to the wells to fill the buckets with water in an attempt to douse the flames. Daily life was punctuated with the traditional rhythm of morning, afternoon and evening prayer; at night the locking of the gates and the boats that travelled up and down watching the canals.

The inhabitants of the ghetto carried out varied tasks; other than the renowned rag traders (*strazzaria*), artisans, small merchants and dye-workers existed; other inhabitants produced oil, wine and kosher food or managed inns for vagrant Jews. One role of high importance in the society was that of doctor. They boasted a good reputation and stood apart from their Catholic colleagues for their way of thinking and religious beliefs, for the differences in their look upon life, general health and illness. They had modern ideas, born of the international influences they had acquired on their continuous, and at times enforced, travels.

Worthy of a mention was the founding of a renowned Jewish publishing house at the beginning of the 16th century, despite numerous difficulties. This publisher was famous not only for the quantity but for the quality of the volumes it produced. Attracted by the favourable political climate of the moment, Jewish intellects came from far and wide (Italy and Europe) with the desire to obtain work in publishing. However, Jews were prohibited from setting themselves up as printers and editors excepting in certain very rare situations; but they were indispensable contributors to the more noted publishing houses of the time: they came and went freely about the city but were always to return to the ghettoes at night.

It was Daniel Bomberg with the aid of Friar Felice de Prato to begin printing works in Hebrew. Bomberg published the *Pentateuch*, a selection from *Prophets* and three subsequent editions of the Jewish Bible (1516–17, 1524–25, 1548), that contained not only the Hebrew text but the Aramaic translation, along with comments from celebrated Jewish critics. Only a few years later this audacious editor, with the permission of the Venetian Senate, gave life to a grandiose project: the twelve-volume *Babylonian Talmud* (1510–23) and the *Palestinian Talmud* (1522–23) along with various prayer volumes commissioned by the numerous members of the community during the diaspora of the era. Tolerance towards these Jewish publications was rapidly changing. In 1551, the Collegio ordered the Executors against Blasphemy to examine the *Talmud* and to advise whether there was cause for incrimination.

In 1553, Venice and the Papacy, in one of their rare harmonious moments, agreed to the fight against heresy and the Jewish culture. The *Talmud* volumes were burnt first in St. Mark's Square then in the Campo dei Fiori, Rome: Venice, in fact, preceded Rome in this action. Only after a period of ten years did the Venetian editors begin once again to publish Jewish books and in 1564 Pius IV once again permitted the reading of *Talmud* with its relative comments; the text, however, was previously censored. In the ghetto's first one hundred year period there was a slow merging process of different Jewish groups: diverse in origins, culture, life experiences, language, dress and even in religious custom. Within the newly constituted ghetto, the most important groups were the so-called German Nationals, consisting of Italian Jews with a hundred year history, both as immigrants from Germanic descent, or more generically referred to as Ashkenazi. Differences were already apparent between the German Jews, used to a hostile environment and themselves untrusting and rigid and the Italian Jews, who were reprimanded for not being sufficiently prepared in the analysis of Jewish texts and for being indolent and Mediterranean. One hundred years later this group had become a minority, outnumbered by the Levantine and Ponentine-Jew merchants of dubious descent. Varied

*Night view
of the square
of the Ghetto Novo.*

sounds could be heard in the ghetto: not only the Hebrew chants and the distorted dialects of the Mediterranean states, but coloured Spanish, Turkish, Portuguese, eastern languages and Greek, not to mention the jargon of certain Polish or German refugees together with the varied Italian dialects. Hebrew was, from what can be gathered, the only common element among the diverse groups present, even if shortly everyone took on the sing-song attributes of the Venetian dialect that created a Jewish-Venetian dialect all of its own—a mixed jargon of both Venetian and Hebrew words. The Sephardites used the Ladino language for awhile (a mixed language formed of antique Spanish and Hebrew elements), the Ashkenazi different forms of Yiddish (language created by a mix of antique German, Hebrew and Polish or Russian elements depending on the origin of the person speaking it) that fell by the wayside rather rapidly. In fact by the end of the 17th century it had practically disappeared. Even the Christian culture and the study of classic texts entered the heavy gates of the ghetto. Bit by bit the Yiddish and Spanish literature was replaced by modern-day fiction, poetry and Latin and Italian essays. Notwithstanding the Jewish view, the merging of the two worlds was becoming more and more evident.

Splendour and decline in the ghetto

The 17th century marked the pinnacle of the ghetto's flourish and contemporaneously the beginning of a new decline. The ghetto was originally inhabited by 700 people, but by 1536 this number had grown to 1,424. This population growth remained constant, so much so, that by the mid-17th century it seems that this had grown to between 4,000 and 5,000 people.

Among these inhabitants, certain well-known personalities, both within and outside the ghetto, stood out: Rabbi Leone da Modena who, over and above the numerous works of religious nature, in 1616–17 compiled a precious collection of customs inherent to the Jewish regulations (*History of Jewish Customs*, 1638); Sara Copio Sullam, poet and guiding spirit, received Jews and non-Jews in her abode in the ghetto, more precisely in the literary lounge. In 1621 she found herself up against a difficult contentious issue with the Archdeacon who accused her of not believing in the immortality of the soul. Of notable importance was the 1638 work of Simone Luzzatto, *Discorso circa il stato de gl'Ebrai et in particolar dimoranti nell'inclita città di Venezia* ("Discussion on the state of the Jews and in particular the residents of the noble city of Venice"), that was written to convince the Venetian government of the usefulness of the Jewish presence in the city and this was backed by factual statements. Luzzatto interpreted the Venetian myth (to which the great Jewish philosophers Isaac Abrabanel and Davide de Pomis had attributed metaphysical connotations) based upon the commercial reality of its time and with the assistance of historical-political considerations.

MANIFESTO
DI
SARRA COPIA
SVLAM HEBREA.

Nel quale è da lei riprouata, e detestata l'opinione negante l'immortalità dell'Anima, falsamente attribuitale dal

SIG. BALDASSARE BONIFACCIO.

Con Licenza de' Superiori.

IN VENETIA, M. DCXXI.
Appresso Giouanni Alberti.

Night view of the square of the Ghetto Novo.

The Manifesto *that relates to the immortality of the soul of* Sara Copio Sullam, *1621.*

The Ponentine community, grown rapidly in number, met with a period of opulence in the 17th century, testified also by the synagogues built by them, the Spanish Schola being the largest and most magnificent of the ghetto. Of the Maran people living in this historical century in Venice, the most illustrious of all was Mosè Zacuto, Spanish born, author of *Tofteh' Aruch* ("Prepared Hell"), in which he outlined the conditions of a sinner, following death, who descends to Hell: it was in fact this poem that landed him the nickname of the "Jewish Dante." The Bubonic Plague that tormented Venice in 1630 was the cause of 50,000 deaths of the 150,000 inhabitants and deeply affected the socio-economic conditions of the city. It was a harsh blow, felt particularly deeply by the Jewish merchants who, until this time, had benefited from the favourable economic international situation and good relationships with the Turks and who were suddenly obliged to suspend import/export to and from the city for reasons of possible infection. They lost enormous quantities of merchandise, considered infected and subsequently burnt and had to pay, together with the German Jews, over 120,000 ducats of extraordinary taxes. In 1645 Venice and the Turks resumed reciprocal hostility which culminated in a strenuous battle over the island of Candia. This island had been subjected to twenty years of Turkish siege. With peace in 1699 came the passing of the island to the Sublime Porte. This long period of crisis had a profound effect on Venice as far as finances and commercial activities were concerned. For the Jews this was accentuated by, on one hand, heavier taxes and gabelle and on the other, a reduction in commerce that diminished their natural role as commercial intermediaries. The poverty that followed increased and placed great pressure on the security banks. The Jewish cultural and religious atmosphere as a result of these difficulties, in the

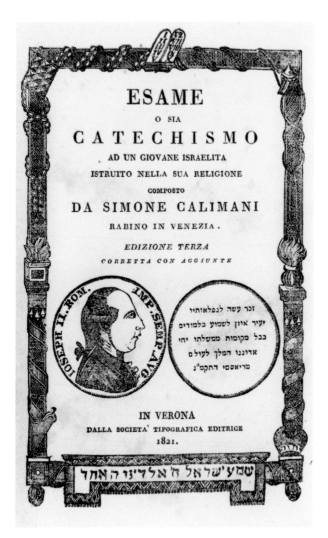

The Catechism
of a Young Israeli
*by Rabbi Simone
Calimani
(1699–1784).*

1660s, sparked enthusiasm and aspirations for the Messiah, guided by the false Messiah Sabbatai Zevi and sustained by numerous messengers arriving from Safed, the most important mystical cultural centre of Palestine.

The renewed religious fervour that had spread across the Mediterranean basin, was quashed with the news that the pseudo-Messiah had converted to Islam and when the prophet of Sabbatai, Nathan of Gaza arrived in Venice in 1668, his visit exacerbated passions and created turmoil.

The Most Serene Republic, meanwhile, had fallen prey to a slow, but irreversible decline and also his hegemony on the Adriatic was soon placed under attack. The peace of Passarowitz, of July 1718, sanctioned the defeat and the disappearance of Venice from the Aegean and the withdrawal from Morea, but acquired above all the significant symbol of two eclipses: not only of Venice but also of the Sublime Porte.

During the years stretching from 1669–1700, the Jewish University, in deference to the decree of the Senate, paid the enormous sum of 800,000 ducats into the coffers of the Most

Serene Prince. On 6 January 1700, the Senate, under pressure from the economic situation and acknowledging the "prompt and devoted resignation" of the heads of the University, declared that the University must deposit, without delay, a further sum of 150,000 ducats. The crisis, in particular that of the security banks, and more in general of the University's finances, practically bled dry during the last thirty years of the 17th century as a result of its onerous financial standing, would have become the norm for many decades to come in Venetian politics, thus creating paradoxical situations that were, until a few years earlier, unthinkable. The Jews, burdened by debts and without property assets, were no longer running the risk of expulsion, in fact their debts acted as a more powerful shield than any of their past riches.

The regulation of 1777 brought with it new restrictions that, nevertheless, did not create too many problems in the ghetto: only a few Jews decided to leave.

The swansong of the relationship between the Most Serene Republic and the Jewish University came about in 1797: very soon both of them would suddenly disappear. In that year, the Republic swayed under the pressure of Napoleon's army; the Jews of the ghetto offered silver and money in a last stand chance of saving the exhausted Venice. On 6 April the Venetian Senate—and this was to prove to be one of its last documents—issued a decree of thanks towards the Jews.

On 12 May 1797 the government abdicated and granted the occupation of the city to the French troops. On 17 May a provisional Municipality was formed who, on 7 July, declared "that the gates to the ghetto were to be lifted in order to remove any signs of separation between the Jewish citizens and the citizens of the city, whereas certain gates should never have been in existence." The enthusiasm of the Jews was extraordinary: in the ghetto square, the inhabitants danced and sang praises to their freedom and to Napoleon. The end of the Most Serene Republic and the fall of the antique gates of the ghetto marked the end of the Jewish University. The history of the ghetto was thus ended, while the history of the Jews, by now citizens of the city, continued to evolve via new situations. The Jews were still not, however, fully entitled citizens, though this would change in the near future. The antiquated security banks were liquidated and the funds obtained were donated to the State, as a contribution from the Jewish community for the foundation of a pawnshop in the lagoon city.

The Venetian Jews following the decline of the ghetto

Austrian troops entered the city on 18 January 1798. The complete civil equality acquired by the Jews by this time revealed itself to be a short-lived dream and they were, until the return of the French in 1806, subjected to some restrictions: they were not able to practice as pharmacists (even though during the end of the Most Serene Republic a few Jewish pharmacists existed) and they were excluded from the Municipal congregation. Notwithstanding these prohibitions, under Austrian rule, the Jews were not so badly off and they benefited from a discrete freedom: they were no longer obliged to pay heavy taxes, nor were they obliged to reside in the ghetto, the gates of which were never restored. They were able to make many choices that were, up until a few years earlier, unimaginable: buy property, set up businesses on their own, enlist in the military forces, enter the public schooling system and work in public office, take part in famous cultural institutions such as the Ateneo Veneto, the Veneto Institute, the Academy of Fine Arts. The "General Fraternity of Worship and Benevolence" was also founded, a self-governing organisation that was to coordinate the activities of the Jewish institutions.

From a curious census carried out at the turn of the century, a very detailed portrait of the social situation in Venice at the time of the ghetto's abolition was revealed: the existence of certain rich families, such as Isacco and Giuseppe Treves', noted bankers and ship-owners that boasted twelve service personnel; or Leon Vita, Jacob Vita and Lazzaro Vivante, merchants, who boasted seventeen employees. Well-to-do families included Marco and Gabriele Malta, Isacco Morpurgo, Beniamino Errera, Abramo Motte and Salomone Curiel. Apparently there were only thirty or so families, for a total of two hundred persons, out of a population of 1,620 that were considered well-to-do or rich. The others were traders, in particular rag traders (strazzaria), labourers, employees of the various Jewish institutions (chazan, janitors and school teachers), a few doctors, pit custodians, one farmer and those who begged for a living. The only rabbi recorded was a certain Abramo Jona from Split, notwithstanding the fact that there were numerous synagogues in the ghetto. This document testifies that the population was relatively poverty stricken, with the poor and the occasional workers largely outnumbering the rich merchants and bankers.

In 1848, in various parts of Italy, rebellions broke out. In Venice, Manin and Tommaseo, who had been previously arrested by the Austrian government, were freed during a mass revolt on 17 March 1848 and were triumphantly carried to St. Mark's Square. A provisional government of the Venice Republic was established, presided over by the same Manin: among the seven signatories certifying the deed one Jew, Leone Pincherle, was present. He was nominated Minister for Agriculture and Trade. The Jews collaborated passionately to this revolt: the more well-to-do were taxed to assist in the defence of Venice's freedom, while many young people enlisted in the artillery of Bandiera and Moro. It was, however, an uneven battle and Venice, depleted by the siege and hunger, was forced to surrender on 28 August 1849. The Austrians were hard to quickly forget the Jewish collaboration towards the Republic of Manin and Tommaseo. They kept strict control over the community: an Austrian guard was even stationed at the religious ceremonies within the synagogues.

In 1866 Venice became an integral part of Italy and the Jews welcomed with enthusiasm and great patriotic pomp the victory and entrance into the city of Vittorio Emanuele II's troops. According to an 1869 census, there were 2,415 Venetian Jews in the city. Of these, 64 percent lived in the ghetto and the surrounding parishes and 23 percent in the St. Mark's area. The well-to-do Jews, part of the medium to high bourgeois, went to live in the centre of the city, while the poorer citizens remained in the ghetto. On the eve of the First World War the Israeli community in Venice had reached 3,000 in number.

At the turn of the 20th century, strong, compact Jewish groups no longer existed, but rather Venetian Jews who were deeply integrated into the life of the city, even if this integration referred more to the bourgeois class than that of the masses. Many families were living outside the ghetto by this time. However the area remained the focal point for community life: there was a kindergarten, a school, a very active club called "Heart and Harmony," while the local clinic had become the Nursing Home. There was, and still is today, a bakery that produced the traditional unleavened bread and desserts. The entire ghetto came to life for each celebration, especially at *Purim*, when the empty clearing in front of the Levantine temple (where a kindergarten now stands) made way for a veritable fair with carnival rides, attractions and sweet stalls. Certain representatives of the community had their names connected to definite achievements: Luigi Luzzatti, who subsequently was elected head of the Italian government, founded the Superior Trade Institute, the well-known Ca' Foscari; Moisè Raffaele Levi founded the Marino Hospice; Michele Treves signed important works, of which the transformation of the aqueduct and the gas company.

The Venetian Jews were naturally active participants in all events of the Italian State and also contributed to World War I. In fact a plaque commemorating the fallen was placed outside the Spanish Schola. In 1938, racial laws fell upon the entire Italian community of Venice, which by then numbered almost 40,000 persons. The Venetian Jews, who made up 1,200 of these, were suddenly discriminated against, alienated from their schools and workplaces even though they were naturally widely integrated with the Catholic community via mixed marriages. Following the Armistice of 8 September 1943, the situation took a turn for the worse: the Germans occupied the city and on 16 September the president of the Jewish community, Giuseppe Jona, committed suicide rather than hand over a list of Jews to the Nazis. During the night of 5 December the Republican Fascist Guard and police headquarters rounded up all Jews in Venice, Lido, Trieste and its islands and Chioggia: over one hundred people were arrested: men, women, children between the ages of three and fourteen. For the entire year of 1944, while war raged on all fronts, Veneto was experiencing a veritable manhunt with a continued threat of persecution and deportation. From summer to autumn 1944 the SS, on orders from Franz Stangi, deported twenty-two guests of the local clinic, twenty-nine patients from the hospitals, the head rabbi of the community (elderly and almost blind), certain psychiatric patients from the hospitals on the islands of San Servolo and San Clemente. Some of these unfortunate deportees were killed in the concentration camps of Riseria di San Sabba in Trieste, others were sent to Auschwitz in Poland. At the end of April 1945 freedom could once again be breathed and Nazi-Fascism was a thing of the past. During these years over two hundred Venetian Jews were deported—only seven survived. Following the war, the community, reduced to a mere 1,000 in number (in 2000 the registered Jews were 420), began to rebuild their social and religious standing and slowly life in the ghetto flourished, firstly with the transfer of the community offices that had, until then, resided in another part of the city, then with cultural initiatives aimed at attracting Jews and non-Jews to the historic sites that are still today visited by tourists from all over the world.

*The portico
of the Ghetto
Vecchio with
the foundations
flooded with
high-water.*

*The main calle
of the Ghetto
Vecchio.*

*The portico
that leads from
the Ghetto Vecchio
to the foundations
of Cannaregio.*

*The holes left
from the hinges
of the gates
to the Ghetto
Vecchio.*

Rio Cannaregio and the Guglie Bridge.

23

The bridge
that leads from the
Ghetto Novissimo
to the Ghetto Novo.

The bridge and
the tall residences
of the Ghetto Novo.

Pages 26 and 27:
the canal
surrounding the
Ghetto Novo.

The monuments to the Holocaust

There are two monuments in the square of the Ghetto Novo in memory of the Holocaust that were erected in different moments. The Holocaust being the extermination of two thirds of the European Jews during the Nazi-Fascist rule between 1938 and 1945.

In 1980 on the wall that rises alongside the Nursing Home, seven bronze bas-reliefs were mounted, work of Lithuanian sculptor and painter Arbit Blatas, who wished to donate these works of art, entitled *Monument to the Holocaust*, to Venice, his adopted city, in memory of his mother who had been deported to a Nazi concentration camp. These seven tablets create a great impact and capture some of the emblematic mo-

ments of the Jewish persecution with both pain and pity; they are entitled *The Deportation, The Night of the Crystals, The Quarry* (as a symbol of hard labour), *The Punishment, Execution in the Ghetto, Rebellion of the Warsaw Ghetto, The Final Solution.*

Together with the support of the Municipality of Venice and thanks to the sculptor's generosity, a further bas-relief was added to the wall years later that encircles the Nursing Home's garden. This bas-relief represents a long train of cattle wagons into which the Jews destined to the concentration camps are pushed with force. Beneath this a wooden plaque was mounted, upon which the names of those Venetian Jews killed and their ages (from two months to eighty) is engraved.

Grand German Schola

Visitors entering the square of the Ghetto Novo, from the portico connecting the latter with the area that consisted of the Ghetto Novissimo, can view on the right a further portico that was once the headquarters of the security banks and where the writing "*banco rosso*" ("red bank") is still evident. To the left, the entrance to the Jewish Museum and the Grand German Schola can be found (1528), next to which the offices and Jewish library are situated, and further on the Canton (1531) and Italian Schola (1571). These were built by the first settlers of the ghetto, the so-called German Nationals, consisting of German Jews, that had arrived in Italy during the 13th and 14th centuries to escape the persecution that had spread through their countries,

and Italian Jews that had come up from the south of the peninsula.

"*Schola*" (or School) is the name the Venetian Jews gave to their places of worship. These were elsewhere referred to as synagogues or temples. The name most probably derives from the Greek word *skol* meaning "confraternity, congregation" that is closest to the Hebrew meaning *beth ha-kenesset* (meeting house) but it could also be connected to the name given to the meeting places of the Venetian confraternity, *scuole* ("schools" – Scuola di San Giorgio degli Schiavoni, Scuola di San Marco etc.). The Jewish synagogues were not like churches in the Catholic community, used exclusively for prayer, but were also places of study and meeting for the

The matroneum and the bimah.

Opposite page: column with Corinthian capital.

community *(kehillah)*. During this ghetto era, administrative seats within the synagogue were elected on an annual basis by the General Assembly of each of the groups (German, Italian, Levantine, Ponentine): the seats were for *parnassim*, general administrators or superintendents; *gabba'im*, secretaries; *gizbar*, treasurer; *chazan*, cantor; *shammash*, sacristan. As with the namesake of the various Venetian institutions, the administrators and employees of the Jewish Schola had various tasks to carry out of an organisational and charitable nature: dress the poor, teach children, cure the ill, bury the dead, redeem slaves, *"maritar donzelle"* (marry off young women), and even take water to the *"infelici"* (unhappy) who did not have running water in their houses.

The Schola all had certain common elements of interior design: the *bimah* or *tevah*, being the pulpit from which the officials preached sermons from the *Torah* (Bible) and other prayer volumes: the *aron ha-kodesc* ("Holy Ark") within which the *Torah* rolls were housed; pews where the men sat and the matroneum, a wing reserved for the women who, by tradition, were separated from the men. Jewish law prohibited the representation of the human figure (believing that it could cause idolatry among the congregation) and therefore paintings and frescoes were not evident; for this reason the synagogue walls were decorated with marble, wooden columns, bronze or silver chandeliers, fabric and curtains and writings (almost always biblical verse). During the 18th and 19th centuries, nevertheless, the influence from the outside world was felt in the artistic arena and objects and paintings were created that represented, among other things, human-like figures. The Venetian synagogues were built on the higher floors of the building, in conformity with

*Detail of the grates
and columns
of the matroneum.*

*The matroneum
and ceiling viewed
through the grates.*

The ceiling and octagonal skylight.   *Detail of one of the wooden decorations.*

that stipulated by the *halacha* (Jewish Law)—to build synagogues in the tallest part of the city in order to be closer to the sky and that they not bear signs of recognition from the exterior to prevent irritating the government of the Republic, who had reluctantly granted permission for their construction in the first place.

These synagogues are, however, so very richly decorated on the inside that, as urged by the *Zohar* (fundamental text of the *Kabbalah*), "the synagogue and its interior design are to be of the utmost beauty." One very important element of Jewish tradition is the lighting, symbol of strength, life and security; for this reason, the synagogues have always boasted large windows through which light may enter to brighten the halls of prayer.

The Grand German Schola was founded soon after the insurgence of the ghetto, by the Ashkenazi Jews and testified in the writing that appears below the cornice: "Grand German Schola of the Holy Community that God may protect them. Amen." From the exterior the Schola is recognisable from the five large arched windows, two of which have been bricked in, while a small *liagò* (apse or aedicule) that marks its presence on the canal. Once upon a time, there was probably a very steep staircase that led from the square of the

Detail of the bimah *pediment.*

Detail of the wooden decorations and a column.

Opposite page: columns and grates of the matroneum.

ghetto directly to the synagogue; these days access is made via a number of staircases that also lead to the Jewish Museum situated on the lower floors of the building.

A plaque, situated above a window on the exterior of the building testifies to the fact that the synagogue was built in 1732; a subsequent and radical restoration of this building was carried out in the 19th century. On the walls of the first staircase, a further plaque testifies that during the years from 1975–79 the synagogue was once again restored by the Italian Committee for Venice and the DKR – Deutscher Koordinierungsrat of Frankfurt. Not much remained, however, of the original building within which, nevertheless, the adaptations of the simple original Ashkenazi structure to the more gaudy elegance of Venetian architecture are evident. This can be seen from the stylistic contrasts and the brilliant chromatic solutions adopted, rendering the whole atmosphere more fascinating.

Through the Renaissance-style door, one enters the hall of prayer that displays a trapezoidal and asymmetric floor plan, rather than the rectangular ones in other synagogues: the elliptic matroneum, sustained by the graceful Rococo columns running the entire parameter of the ceiling softens this irregular aspect of the floor plan. An octagonal chandelier gives depth to the hall. The matroneum in its origins must have included a type of canopy above the arch, as can be seen in the Levantine synagogue of Ancona. Subsequently, most probably during the 18th century, this was moved and rebuilt along one side of the long hall, in keeping with the two large Sephardite synagogues (the Levantine Schola and the Spanish Schola).

The *bimah* (or *tevah*) must once have been the centrepiece of the hall, as was common among the Ashkenazi synagogues

A bronze chandelier.   *The* aron
*with the Ten
Commandments
carved into the door.*

The pews and the bimah *and, to the right, detail of pew backs.*

Opposite page: the square of the Ghetto Novo as viewed from the window of the German Schola.

and as can be testified by the empty space lacking decoration at the centre of the floor; during the restorations of 19th century this was moved to one of the shorter sides of the hall with the scope of recuperating the bifocal structure typical of Venetian synagogues.

When positioned at the centre of the hall, the *bimah* was of an octagonal shape, a characteristic documented in the French and German parchments. Its move entailed the closure of two windows, the partial covering of the Ten Commandments, the elimination of two columns and the addition of two pieces of cornice and one of balustrade; these modifications gave the illusion that the *bimah* was trapezoidal, without detracting from its gracefulness.

From the opposite side of the hall, the elegant Renaissance *aron* (Holy Ark), of small dimension, surmounted by the Corinthian pediment decorated in gold plate and bright Baroque elements, is flanked by the seats utilised by the *parnassim* (synagogue administrators) and by two large windows situated above four steps in red Venetian marble, upon which the name of the donor and the year of construction is inscribed: 1666. The doors of the *aron* display the Ten Commandments inlayed in mother-of-pearl, that are also evident on the walls in marmorino plaster (lower quality material, as was dictated by the Most Serene Republic): even the writing that covered all the walls was an Ashkenazi decorative element that was subsequently adopted by Italian synagogues. The gold decorative elements and the red curtains, characteristic of Venetian synagogues, were most probably inspired by the Temple of Jerusalem or at least from pictures of same handed down through tradition. The prayer pews, simple and severe in their style, contrast the pomp and splendour of the Baroque furnishings.

Jewish Museum

The Jewish Museum, situated in two large rooms on the first floor of the building that houses the German Schola, was opened in 1955; subsequently restored and in need once more of restoration or transfer in order to be able to display more objects.

The collection of material is represented, as in all Jewish museums, by synagogue furnishings and objects relating to the various Jewish celebrations and customs, some still in use today: there are not, therefore, a large number of objects, but their fine workmanship is most evident and the origins of the objects and the names of their donors, together with the material utilised, is great testimony to the lives and history of the Venetian Jews.

Silver Chanukiah *(nine branch lamp), Russia, beginning of 20th century.*

Ketubah *(matrimonial contract), Lugo, Romania, 1775.*

בסימנא
טבא
ובמזל"א
מיל"א

מצא

זה מצא טוב

בששי בשבת אחד עשר יום לחדש סיון שנת חמשת אלפים המ[ש]
מאות ושלשים והכש לבריאת יערלם למנין שאנו מנין בו פה לונ כרתא
דירבא יזל נזר כינו וסינטירנו ומי באירת בא הבחור הנעים כמראברהם
יצובי הכינתר ר יצחק דינא זל ואמר לה להבתולה הצנועה מרת אסתר
בתריתא תבא בת המפואר כבר מרדכי סנגאליא יצו חוי ליל/אנתו כדת
משה וישראל ואנא בסייעתא דשמיא אפלה ואוקיר ואזון ואפרנם יתיכי
כהלכת גברין יהודאין דפלחין ומוקרין וזנין ומפרנסין לנשיהון בקושטג-
ויהיבנא ליכי מהר בתוליכי כסף זוזי מאתן דחזו ליכי ומזוניכי וכסותיכי
וספוקיכי ומיעל לותיכי כארח כל ארעא וצביאת מרת אסתר כלתא בתולתא
דא תבא והות ליה לאנתו לכמר אברהם יצו חתן דנן ודא נדוניא דהנעלת
ליה כבי אבוה עשרין ליטרין של כסף צרוף וצבי כמר אברהם יצו חתן
דנן ואוסף לה מדיליה כמכונה עשרין ליטרין של כסף צרוף נמצא סכום
כתובתא דא בין נדוניא ובין תוספא ארביען ליטרין של כסף צרוף בר
ממאתן זוזי דחזו לה וכך אמר כמר אברהם יצו חתן דנן אחריות כתובתא
דא קבלית עלי ויגל ירתי בתראי להתפריעא מן כל שפר ארג נכסין וקנענן
דאית לי תחות כל שמיא דקנאי ודיעתיד אנא למקנא נכסין דאית להון
אחריות ואגבן דלית להון אחריות רי להון כלהון אחראין ויערבאין למפרע
מנהון כתובתא דא יזך גמירא ואפילו מן גלימא דעל כתפי בהיי ולבתר
חיי מן יומא רנן ולעלם וקבל יעליו כבר אברהם יצו חתן דנן חמר שטר
כתובתא דא כחמר כל שטרי כתובות דנהינין בבנות ישראל הבתולות
הצניעות והכשירות דלא כאסכפתא ודלא כטופסי דשטרי וקנינא אנן סהדי
דהתימי לתהא מן היקר כמר אברהם יצו חתן דנן לזכות הבתולה הצנועה
מרת אסתר כלהא דא תבא יזל כל מאי דכתיב ומפרש ליעיל במנ/
דכשר לבקנא ביה והכל שריר וקים

נעם תיכות אחד עשר יום דעל הדרי דרן קימיהון והכל שריר וקים

Rather than describe each single object, we prefer to explain the significance and utilisation of these objects. Many of them are ornaments to the *Sefer Torah* ("Law Book"): the antique biblical text, written on parchment and fixed to two sticks that permit the unravelling for reading. When not in use, the *sefer* is enclosed in a precious fabric casing *(meil)* from which the two sticks protrude. A silver crown *(ataroth)*, symbol of the *Torah*, is placed onto this casing together with two silver tip covers *(rimmonim)* for purely ornamental purposes. Occasionally the *sefer* is adorned with a plaque or medallion *(tas)*, again for purely ornamental purposes, upon which the name of the donor and some biblical verses are inscribed. These rolls are kept within a gilt wooden box *(tiq)* for ease of transport. The following articles also form part of the temple's furnishings: *parocheth* (drapes or curtains) that are hung before the *aron* to recall the curtain that enclosed the Holy Ark with the Laws of the Temple of Jerusalem; the key to open this *aron* and the pointed hand indicator *(yad*, meaning hand), that the officials used for following the text—often in finely worked silver; the embroidered fabric bags for the *talled* (cloak used by the men) and *siddur* (prayer book); the precious book bindings; the chalice used to drink the wine for the consecration of the Sab-

bath and other celebrations; the jug and basin used by the Levi to wash the hands of the *Cohanim* (priest) prior to pronouncing the benediction.

Many other objects are connected to the traditional Jewish festivals: the most important of all being the *menorah*, the seven-branch Sabbath lamp (depicting the seven days of the week), symbol of the Jewish people. The *portabessamim* (perfume/spice bottles) that were of ornate design and workmanship and in various shapes, utilised during *avdala* (separation), the benediction that celebrates the coming of the *Shabbat* (Sabbath or Saturday, which is separated from the rest of the week).

The *channukiah* is the nine branch lamp that is lit for eight evenings leading up to the Sabbath (the ninth branch being the *shammash* or servant, utilised purely for lighting the other eight) during *Chanukah*. This celebration is in memory of the rebellion of the Maccabei brothers (164 BCE), who had succeeded in exiling the Syrian Antiochus Epiphanes, who had conquered the country and transformed the Holy Temple into a pagan one.

When the Temple was finally re-consecrated it was discovered that only one drop of precious oil remained to re-light the *ner tamid* (eternal flame). This drop miraculously last-

To the left of the photo, the tiq *(the gilt wooden box that housed the* Sefer Torah*); in the background,* *the glass cabinets containing the* parocheth *(drapes, curtains) utilised to decorate the synagogue* *and the* meilim *(fabric casings) utilised to cover the* Torah *parchments.*

ed for eight days, the time required to procure other oil. The *shofar* is a ram or mutton horn that was once blown to gather the population. This custom is repeated today during the *Rosh Hashanah* (Jewish New Year), *Kippur* and *Sukkot* festivals. The *megilloth* of Ester is a long, rolled parchment enclosed in a thick, silver engraved casing. This parchment is read at *Purim* and narrates the story of Ester, wife of the King of Persia, Assuero, who saved the Jewish population from the threat of destruction at the hands of the treacherous minister Amman: during this festival, that is a veritable Jewish fair, traditional sweets are eaten and spinning tops are played. Some of these, in silver, are displayed at the Jewish Museum. Decorative silver and ceramic plates are utilised during *Pesach*, the celebration of the freedom attained following the escape from Egypt and during the dinner called *seder*, a book is read that contains the sequence of events *(haggada)* and unleavened bread and other customary foods are eaten.

Other objects relate to Jewish family life, such as the *shaddaim* (pendants inscribed with the attributes of God) that are hung above babies' cradles, the illuminated *kettubah* (matrimonial contracts) and the *mezzuzot* (cases enclosing a small rolled prayer parchment), that are hung from the door jambs of the Jewish houses.

Ataroth *(silver crown for the* Torah *rolls), Venice, beginning of the 18th century.*

Rimmonim *(silver ornaments utilised to cover the stick tips upon which the* Torah *is rolled), Turkey (?), 16th century.*

Silver portabessamim *(perfume/spice bottles), Moscow, 19th century (?), donated by Paolo Alazrachi.*

Canton Schola

The Canton Schola (1531–32) is situated in the square of the ghetto near the German Schola and is also of Ashkenazi custom. It is recognisable from the outside by a small domed skylight, and from the canal by a *liagò* (or *diagò* apse or aedicule on the façade, typical element of Venetian architecture) and by five windows. The name Canton derived most probably from the family that financed its construction, or a group of families connected together via one or more elements (i.e.: Canton) or certain customs, or from the corner position of the Schola itself (in Venetian dialect the word *canton* means corner) or alternatively because the Schola was built by Ashkenazi Jews of French origin, maybe Provençal. One ancient topographical map published in Paris during the 17th century describes the ghetto as *Canton des Juifs* and in archived documents it can be read that this synagogue followed the French-Ashkenazi customs that had also spread through Piedmont.

The bimah *and, above, detail of the wooden decorations.*

Detail of a
decorative column.

On pages 50 and 51:
Shell-shaped apse
surmounting the
bimah.

The synagogue, although restored in various moments throughout history (the atrium and stairwell were restored in 1859), has not lost its symmetry or its original linear form. A plaque is placed above the external entrance portal that quotes: "Year of construction 5292 [1532] of the Synagogue of the Holy Canton Community."

The hall boasts a rectangular floor plan, with the *aron* and the *bimah* positioned on the shorter sides of the room and the pews along the longer sides: the bifocal attributes, adopted by all Venetian synagogues, could be a connection to the synagogues of Carpentras and Cavaillon and thus lean towards the French origin of its founders. On each of the longer walls of the hall five windows are evident: those on the western side of the hall faced the canal while the eastern windows look over a narrow opening and have since been closed over; once all ten windows were exposed and the hall would have benefited from an ample illumination and the prayers would have been heard all across the ghetto square. The *bimah* is in the late-Renaissance style (the date inscribed on the step is 1672) and is framed by a semi-elliptic arch of Rococo style and supported by two pairs of columns engraved with plaited branches and ornate, elegant Pompeiian-style motifs, while the five wooden steps give it a raised position in the hall.

The *aron*, boasting detailed and valuable gilt carvings, is flanked by two Corinthian columns and seats of the *parnassim*, surmounted by a split pediment through which centre light filters via the coloured glass of the windows positioned behind, creating a halo effect around the Ark. A number of gold framed paintings can be noted around the walls of the hall depicting religious subjects, pleasing to the eye but not of great value: Moses, who caused water to gush from rock, a view of Jerusalem, the sacrificial altar, Jordan, the passage over the Red Sea.

The window behind the aron.

The external façade and skylight.

A Corinthian capital and, below, detail of the decorative centre of the ceiling.

Opposite page: the pews and bimah *(above) and the* aron *(below).*

Italian Schola

The Italian Schola is recognised by the five large windows that face onto the ghetto square, surmounted by a coat of arms upon which the following is written: "Holy Italian Community: 1575" and by the small dome that overhangs the pulpit. This synagogue was built by a group made up of Italian Jews of Roman origin, small time lenders and rag traders *(strazzaria)*, and therefore not in any favourable financial position to create a synagogue of great wealth such as the German Schola. Nevertheless, this synagogue has a very strong cultural identity. The Italian Jews, regardless of the fact that they had not constituted a separate "national" group from that of the Germans, to which they formed part, maintained slightly different customs to those of the Ashkenazi Jews.

Cassuto hypothesises on the existence of a smaller Renaissance synagogue, prior to this one, as a cultural refuge for the first Italian Jews settling into the ghetto in 1516. It was most probably built following the style of the Renaissance synagogues of Rome, no longer in existence today and replaced by 19th-century places of worship. This original school was more than likely situated on the first floor of the

building to then be transferred to the higher floors at a later stage where it may still be visited today. The steep staircase that leads to this place of worship was most probably built during the 18th-century restorations, as the portico and two pillars on the building's façade, still visible today, are of a more Roman style than Venetian. These stairs lead to another wider staircase and entrance. This stairwell boasted an atrium where a fountain was placed for the washing of hands, together with a coffer for the collection of offerings and a plaque commemorating the restoration that took place in 1739. The stairs lead to an entrance of which the function is not known (this is a typical characteristic of synagogues in Eastern Europe but not of those in Italy) and consequently to the hall of prayer, that maintained the typical Venetian rectangular structure, even if not very elongated.

The *bimah* and the *aron* are positioned on the shorter sides of the hall. As the difference between the long and short walls of the hall is not very evident, the impression of entering into a narrow route through two flames, common to the other synagogues, is not as accentuated. Rather a feeling is attained of entering into a square-shaped environ-

*Opposite page:
one of the
decorative wall
paintings. On this
particular one,
in the centre,
as with the others,
a dark stone is
evident upon
which an acrostic
inscription
indicates the name
of Avraham
to whom peace
is requested;
to the right, the
matroneum.*

*To the right:
the* bimah *and
underneath
the aron.*

ment permitting an entire view of the ambience in one go. The *aron*, of valuable workmanship, is decorated by Corinthian columns with a canopy positioned overhead in the Baroque style and surrounded by a balustrade of wooden columns.

More imposing is the *bimah*, elevated one and a half metres from the hall floor by eight steps and placed before a polygonal apse characterised by three coloured bands and enclosed by a fourth column bearing Corinthian capitals. Above the *bimah* an octagonal skylight can be seen that captures light from above, especially so at sunset. The ceiling, delimited by a Renaissance frame is one of the most antique parts of the hall and recalls the church of Santa Marcuola, building from which the artist more than likely got his inspiration. The dark wooden coverings, the beautiful Dutch candelabras, the Renaissance pews, the gilt inscriptions in the dark stone that date back to the 19th century and the grates surrounding the matroneum (moved in relation to their original position beside the *bimah*) provide this small synagogue with a severe but at the same time harmonious appearance.

At the synagogue's exit, on the wall that marks the end of the square, a small hole can be seen, these days stopped up, for offerings to the synagogue (in Hebrew called *zedaqah*, meaning justice). This hole is one of the few remaining of the many that were spotted around the area in days gone by.

The aron *flanked by the dark stone pictures with the gilt inscriptions.*

Levantine Schola

From the square of the Ghetto Novo and by continuing to the left a small bridge is reached where a long calle, surrounded by a network of smaller calle (Calle Barucchi, from the Hebrew *Baruch* "blessed," Calle del Forno, Calle and Corte dell'Orto and Corte Scala Matta) appears. This area is known as the Ghetto Vecchio. Two more spacious synagogues were built in the Ghetto Vecchio: the Levantine Schola (1541) and the Spanish Schola (1584?)—one in front of the other and located at the end of the main street in a small clearing called "delle Scole."

The Levantine Schola was built contemporaneously with the granting of residency to the vagrant Eastern traders, to whom permission was granted by the government of the Most Serene Republic to construct a building that far differed from the others. The traders decided to build an ample and striking synagogue "almost as a demonstration, together with the architectural choices, the wealth of the nation

and the complete Levantine style and desire for all things grandiose and magnificent" (Umberto Fortis, *The Ghetto on the Lagoon*, Venice 1988).

The Levantine Schola is one of the most easily recognisable synagogues even today as it is free-standing and boasts a polygonal aedicule with a shell-shaped roof, called *liagò*, more evident from the façade. The two façades, decorated by a smooth rustic finish on its base and mirrored objects of varied shapes and sizes on the upper part, are very similar to those of certain Venetian palaces of the 17th century, such as Labia Palace and Savorgnan Palace in the neighbouring parish of San Geremia.

These boasted three consecutive windows protected by grates on the ground floor and large windows ending in arches in all their splendour on the upper floor where the hall of prayer was situated. The external and internal structure of this synagogue bears traces of the Venetian influx and in particular

The bronze chandeliers before the aron.

Opposite page: one of the semicircular staircases that lead to the bimah.

*Above and on
opposite page:
the* aron *and
the pews.*

*In the foreground:
a* talled *(prayer
cloak) draped over*

*a pew; in the
background:
the* bimah.

the style of the great architect Longhena. According to the architect David Cassuto, numerous architectural elements such as the cornices around the windows, the stone bands running around the façade, the cornices upon which the roof is constructed and even the grates on the windows, can all be found in the works of Longhena and his school, in particular the Flangini College at San Giorgio dei Greci. Today the main entrance to the synagogue is reached via the calle, while the door to the square of the ghetto gives access to the Luzzatto Schola. The entrance has been moved with respect to the aedicule overhead and the symmetry of the façade is compromised. For this reason it can be deduced that once upon a time the entrance facing the square was more than likely the main one.

From the atrium present on the ground floor of the building, access can be made to the Luzzatto Schola on the right; to the left a staircase is evident that divides into two smaller staircases both leading to the hall of prayer. A further steeper staircase leads to the matroneum situated on the next level.

The hall is rectangle in shape, with the *bimah* and the *aron* positioned one facing the other on the shorter sides and the matroneum on one of the longer sides. The wooden *bimah*, of

unnatural beauty is the most elaborate of all the *bimah* in the Venetian synagogues, and closes the apse surmounted by a shell-shaped dome that protrudes on the outside of the building *(liagò)* and recalls the similar apses that can be found on the basilica of St. Peter in Rome.

Even the tall tortile columns, richly engraved with elaborate motifs of flowers and fruit that support the pulpit *(bimah)* recall the columns of Bernini in the Vatican basilica, from which inspiration was most probably taken. The motifs on the tortile columns are not estranged from Venetian secular art of the 17th century; they can be found in certain theatrical sceneries and in the grand allegory of *Pax veneta* painted by Veronese for the hall of the High Council in the Ducal Palace, "where the most serene Divinity rises above the clouds over the people and the city, framed by two powerful tortile columns that recall the Solomonic columns of St. Peter's in Rome" (Ennio Concina in *The City of the Jews*, Venice 1991).

The tortile columns of the Solomone temple had actually entered into the iconography of western art that, up until mediaeval times, was identified by the symbol of the columns of the Temple of Jerusalem and as such often appeared in the miniature Jewish paintings, such as the beautiful 18th-century

Opposite page: details of one of the staircases that leads to the bimah.

To the right: one of the tortile columns that support the bimah.

Pages 68 and 69: tortile column detail.

ketubah conserved at the Correr Museum in Venice.

The cornice of the *bimah* opens out as it nears the ceiling so as to form a single decorative element extending to the walls. The ceiling (recently restored) presents rich wooden decorations, especially in the ornate central rose in accordance with the traditions of the Venetian palaces. Access to the *bimah*, much higher than the hall's actual level, is obtained via two elegant semicircular staircases. On the opposite side of the hall, the *aron*, flanked by sobering dark marble columns and Corinthian capitals, is encircled by polychrome marble columns and a bronze gate.

A double tympanum closes the central part of the Ark; on the higher one a script in gold leaf on a black background can be found: "I will bow down toward Thy Holy Temple, and give thanks unto Thy name" (Psalm 138:2).

The Ten Commandments are inscribed into the doors of the *aron* and the date 5543 [1782]. Silver lamps hang from the ceiling and beautiful Dutch bronze chandeliers that together with the candelabras situated beside the *aron* enrich and liven up the hall, within which chromatic contrasts are already apparent between the red of the fabric coverings and curtains and the dark hue of the wood.

The structure of the Schola is typically Renaissance, even if the interior was restored in the centuries that followed. The beautiful *bimah* dates back to that time. Tradition would have it that this synagogue was created by the famous sculptor Andrea Brustolon (1662–1732) from Belluno. He was active in Venice and was in fact one of Longhena's students; but no evidence of his participation has been documented. It is clear, however, that a strong connection existed, as can be seen in all the architectural elements and the instilled sense of unity in the building, at the hand of only one possible artist who was surely a non-Jew. This person had to adapt to Jewish demands and laws and create a precious work of art counting only on the architectural elements, decorations and furnishings at hand, without the opportunity of availing of the pictures and frescoes that enriched the palaces and churches of Venice.

Opposite page:
the aron.

Above: the richly
decorated ceiling.

One of the
semicircular
staircases that lead
to the bimah.

The interior
of the hall of prayer
as seen from
the matroneum.

Opposite page:
the bimah.

Luzzatto Schola

Apart from the five main synagogues, other places of worship and study were present in the ghetto that were smaller in size: the Luzzatto Schola, the Mesullanim Schola, the Cohanim Schola, the Midrash Vivante and the Midrash Leone da Modena, nearly all dating back to the 17th century—era in which the ghetto was flourishing. The Cohanim Schola was situated by the bridge that leads to Ghetto Novissimo, near the security banks, but was demolished at the end of the 19th century and all its furnishings transferred to the ground floor of the Spanish Schola. The Mesullanim Schola, situated near the bridge that leads to Ghetto Novo, was also demolished and its furnishings transferred to the small building next door, where the *mikvah* (customary baths) can be found. Where the 19th-century Midrash Vivante once stood, in the main calle of the Ghetto Vecchio, a shop is now present, while that of Leone da Modena, recently restored, has been transformed into the rabbi's offices.

In a small hall situated on the ground floor of the Levantine Schola, from which access is made via the clearing called "Campiello delle Scole," the Luzzatto Schola stands as it has done since the middle of the 19th century. It was previously situated in the Ghetto Novo square beside the Nursing Home and near to the bridge of Rio San Girolamo. Following the Napoleonic conquest and the pulling down of the gates of the ghetto, the entire area adjacent to the bridge was destroyed and the furnishings of the small Schola were moved elsewhere. The Schola was restored following the Second World War with projects commissioned by the Save Venice Committee in memory of Resy and Bruno Luzzatto, who had emigrated to the USA due to the racial laws of the time. The synagogue retains the typical Renaissance aspects of its origins, as can be seen by the heavy wooden beams of the ceiling, the placement of writings on the walls and the furnishings themselves, which remind us of a small Venetian building: the Scuola di San Giorgio degli Schiavoni. The small hall, bearing the characteristic rectangular floor plan, does not have a matroneum, as its only function is that of a place of study. The *aron*, perhaps the most antique of all the ghetto, is surrounded by four columns that reach up to simple architraves and a balustrade made of 19th-century columns. The caisson ceiling and the pictures adorning the higher parts of the walls give the hall a classic tone of sobriety.

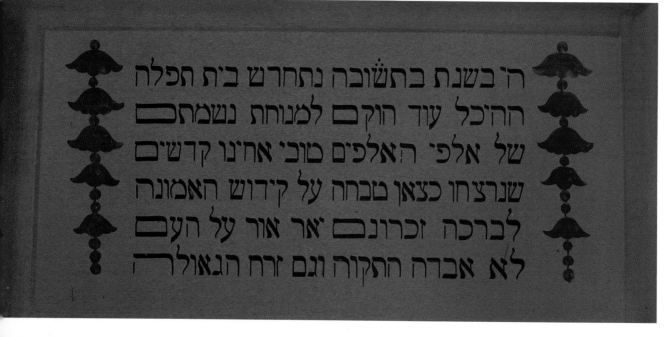

ה׳ בשנת בתשובה נתחדש בית תפלה
ההיכל עוד הוקם למנוחת נשמתם
של אלפי האלפים טובי אחינו קדשים
שנרצחו כצאן טבחה על קידוש האמונה
לברכה זכרונם יאר אור על העם
לא אבדה התקוה וגם זרח הגאולה

One of the poems praising God that adorns the walls.

Brass chandelier.

Opposite page: the aron.

Spanish Schola

The Spanish Schola, the most immense and imposing of all the Venetian synagogues, dates back to halfway through the 16th century (probably 1584). The Jews and Marans of Spanish origin that had landed in Venice gathered together and initially formed a school where their children could recuperate the traditions lost by their fathers when they had abandoned Judaism. A document circulated in 1582 speaks of "a school that hosts foreigners," being a place equipped to host vagrants; other documents of the time demonstrate an attention to detail with regards to the pedagogical aspects of the school and the diligence of the administrators in offering an orthodox education to the children, more than likely to prevent heretic diversions. It is highly probable that during the first ten years of their presence in the city, these crypto-Jews and Marans of dubious origin were not willing to publicly display their customs but preferred the smaller study halls that formed the nucleus of the Schola, that was to become the last built and most impressive synagogues of the ghetto. The Ponentine nationals who built this synagogue were economically, numerically and culturally strong, resulting with the passing of the centuries, that they became the dominant group. So much so that, at the beginning of the 20th century the Ashkenazi customs were once and for all abandoned. The only customs (minhag) that are still followed by the Venetian Community are those of the Sephardite Jews.

The building was built onto and completely modified—more than likely between 1635 and 1657—in accordance with the

The hall of prayer viewed from the bimah.

The wrought iron gate and the staircase leading to the hall of prayer.

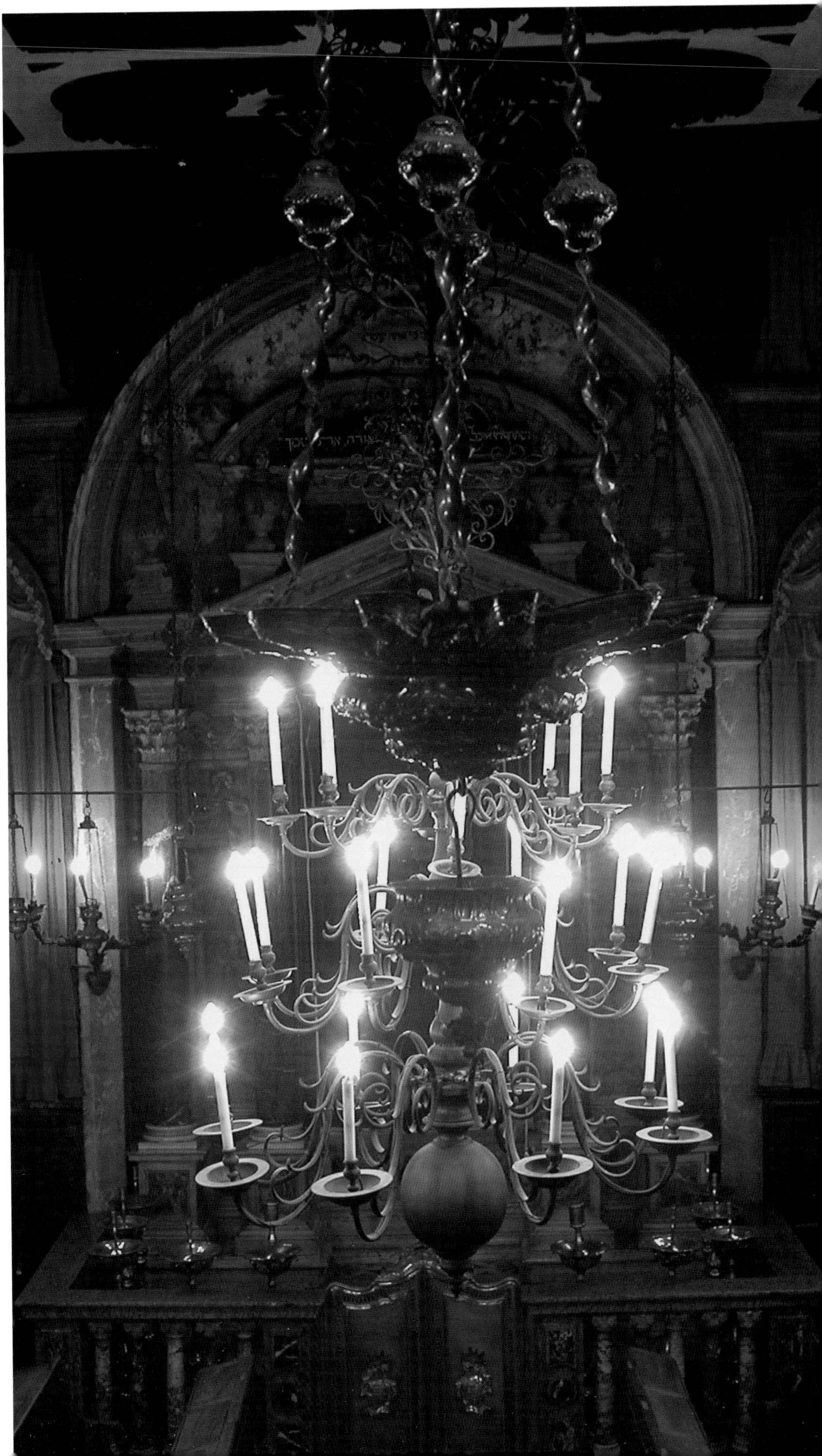

One of the Dutch chandeliers and in the background, the aron.

traditions and work of Baldassarre Longhena, the greatest Venetian architect of that time. It is this restoration that recalls the late Baroque architectural characteristics and style that can still be admired today. Some of the modifications made at the end of the 19th century, during which an organ was introduced to the synagogue (a sign of great assimilation to the costumes and traditions that did not form part of Judaism) and a raised enclosure was built around the *aron*, took away from the initial harmony of the hall. This was returned to its original state with the complete restoration carried out between 1980 and 1983, when the organ was removed and the antique *bimah* put back in its original position.

The less than striking external façade is horizontally divided into two parts by a stone strip that separates the lower part from the higher large arched windows. A marble commemorative plaque stands out below the windows dedicated to the Jews killed in the concentration camps. The synagogue is hidden behind a beautiful wooden door with a classical pediment from whereby you may enter a large atrium housing a small fountain for hand washing. Along with the fountain, numerous commemorative plaques dot the walls. A door leads off from the left-hand side of the atrium to a small hall that houses the furnishings from the Schola Cohanim, demolished during the 19th century; at the end of the atrium two doors can be seen, one of which leads to a small 18th-century *sukkot* (a small hut built during the celebration of *Sukkot* in memory of the Jews' travels in the desert, when they were forced to sleep in tents or huts and eat manna). The other door leads to a steep staircase that takes one up to the matroneum. To the right of the atrium a wide staircase, enclosed by a wrought iron gate, leads to

Interior of the synagogue and below, the bimah.

Parocheth *(drapes that decorate the* bimah) *during the celebration of* Rosh Hashanah *(New Year), donated by Shelomo, Ancona, in 5621 [1861].*

the cultural hall of the synagogue. The simplicity of the exterior contrasts the vastness, wealth and theatrical scenery of the hall that is today one of the most beautiful buildings and theatres of Venice. The floor plan is, as usual, rectangular and as always, the hall is dominated by the *aron* and the *bimah* connected by the long rows of pews and the wooden coverings running behind. The rest of the walls are dominated by alternating columns and impressive windows. The *aron*, decorated by polychrome marble and four black-striped marble columns seems "a nearly identical copy of the main altar of the chapel of the patriarch Cardinal Francesco Vendramin at San Pietro al Castello that was being worked on in 1633" (Ennio Concina). This is contained in the triangular tympanum upon which the Law Tablets were placed, surmounted by a sky-blue painted strip and an Ark upon which is written in gold letters: "Know who you find before you." On the door of the ark the Ten Commandments are engraved, a verse from the Psalms and the date: 1755. The space dedicated to the *aron* is closed via a small gate with wooden columns and is surrounded by bronze candelabras. Besides the steps of the *aron* a small plaque commemorates the event that occurred on 29th of the Av month of 5609 (17th August 1849) when an Austrian bomb was dropped

very close to the synagogue. The inscription, dictated by Rabbi Lattes reads: "Here a bomb was sunk, falling into the abyss, it did not cause damage, it passed with violence but did not judge." Even today, on the last Friday of every Av month "Bomb Friday" is remembered.

The *bimah*, flanked by two marble columns with Corinthian capitals, is surrounded by two short wooden staircases that enclose the posterior section of the vast sky-blue dome placed upon a polygonal apse. The incredibly high ceiling is decorated with elaborate wooden carvings: an idea not far removed from that utilised at the Palazzo Pesaro and in the oratory of San Nicolò dei Greci. Underneath this ceiling, the elliptic matroneum, decorated by balustrade and small wooden columns forming part of the architectural concept of the building, seems to link all elements of the hall together and offers a classic example of Venetian Baroque style. The large Dutch chandeliers, bronze torches, silver lamps (*sessandei* in Venetian dialect from the Latin *cicendelum*, vagrant light), the vast red curtains covering the windows and in certain times of the year, the *parocheth* (curtains) and precious fabrics that adorn the *aron* and other parts of the temple all add to this refined and theatrical quality.

Plaster decorations on the bimah's *dome.*

The pews with the wooden screen that separates the section designated to

women from when the matroneum was closed for restoration.

The pews for prayer and the aron; *below, the hall as viewed from the matroneum.*

Silver lamp
in front of the aron.

Opposite page:
the aron.

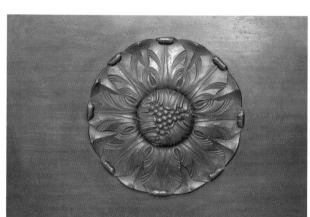

One of the
buttresses that
support the bimah.

Two wooden
decorations
of the bimah.

The Law Tablets on
the aron's pediment.

Opposite page:
the aron.

The matroneum and the hall of prayer as seen from the matroneum.

Silver lamps.

Jewish Cemetery

The Jewish Cemetery of the Lido

In 1386 the Venetian government granted the Jews spread across the Veneto territory a strip of land at San Nicolò on the Lido Island for a cemetery to bury their dead. This land, with the exception of a brief period of time when the grant was suspended for reasons of war during the 17th and 18th centuries, belonged to a small group of Jews who had settled in the ghetto. In fact this piece of land was frequently referred to as "House of Jews," even in maps of the Lido.

From antique times the only grave that remains is that of a certain "Samuel, son of Dr. Shimshon" dating back to 1389. Many other tombstones were lost because the area, originally vast, was withdrawn over the centuries to make way for excavation, fortification and road works that forced the Jews to give up part of the area granted them and to move away from the banks of the lagoon. Many graves disappeared under layers of earth or were even destroyed; some tombstones, removed from the original burial place can still be found in the small piece of land measuring 3,000 square metres called the Ancient Cemetery that covers only a small area in relation to that of the original one. Towards 1774, the Republic granted

The Ancient Cemetery of the Lido prior to recent restoration.

the Jews an adjacent area, of no military interest, of approximately 35,000 square metres that became the New Cemetery. This is still in use today.

Following the demise of the Republic, the Ancient Cemetery was left to abandon, thick with trees and tangled shrubs from which the white Istrian tombstones sprouted giving way to wild, romantic connotations. Many well-read Europeans, such as Johann Wolfgang Goethe, George Byron, Percy Shelley and George Sand, were mesmerised by the atmosphere of this cemetery that became the destination of many an expedition or the inspiration for their poetic licence.

At the beginning of the 20th century the Lido was becoming a tourist attraction: grand hotels were being built, such as the national Target Shooting Palace in the San Nicolò quarter. The Ancient Cemetery was enclosed by a brick wall to render it less visible to the tourists and sealed with a gate made of Istrian stone. A path was created that from the main gate led to the centre of the field, where an impressive marble obelisk was erected having little to do with the atmosphere. Between 1925 and 1929 a road was built that ran alongside the lagoon. Various other excavation works were carried out during which over six hundred higgledy-piggledy tombstones were revealed, evidently removed from the preceding graves. The architect Guido Sullam, who had created the gate of the New Cemetery, catalogued these tombstones and drew up a map of

Ancient Cemetery: small coat of arms for the Cividal and Merari families representing Samson fighting the lion .

the cemetery, while Rabbi Ottolenghi and Vice-Rabbi Pacifici set about deciphering the inscriptions that had eroded over the years. Many tombstones were deposited in the New Cemetery and only in 1993 did restoration begin in part under the direction of the engineer Mario Cherido.

In the Ancient Cemetery, recently cleared of overgrowth and put in order, remaining tombstones date back to the 17th and 18th centuries. Most of them are vertically placed slabs; during the 18th century, nevertheless, some families began to utilise sarcophagi, of which very often only the covers remained. Numerous tombstones bear engravings of Gentile symbols belonging to families of Spanish hidalgos or Portuguese fidalgos or other symbols utilised solely for the purpose of distinguishing one family from the next. Some of these are clearly identifiable, such as the blessing hands of the Cohens (priests) and the jug and basin of the Levis (who, as tradition would have it, had to wash the priests' hands). Other families were inspired by biblical motifs, such as the crown (symbol of the *Torah*), the *shofar* (ram horn that, in this case, signifies resurrection), a palm frond (symbol of benediction),

explorers carrying a bunch of grapes (symbol of Israel). Others utilise iconographic symbols that are deciphered to reveal the name of the deceased, such as an angel for the D'Angeli family, three French lilies for the Sarfatti family (*Zarfàt* is the Hebrew name from France), a staircase for the Sullum family (*sulàm*, staircase). Other very common decorative elements can be found in the climbing lion and the star images; of the more elaborate and original symbols we recall the rooster with an ear of corn surmounted by a moon or half-moon for the Luzzatto family; the stag carrying the classic conical wicker basket for Saraval; Samson fighting the lion for Cividal and Merari. Most of the epigraphs are written in Hebrew, others in Jewish Spanish but in Hebrew characters. Others bear the name of illustrious personalities such as Elia Levita (1472–1549) grammatist and editor of Jewish publications, the great Rabbi and scholar Leone da Modena (1571–1648), the poet Sara Copio Sullam (1592–1641), the historian and scholar Simone Luzzatto (1583–1663), Ponentine Daniele Rodriga (?–1603), the port captain from Split and many more or less recognised Jewish personalities from the Venetian ghetto.

Tombstones in the Ancient Cemetery.

Coats of arms representing two families: the blessing hands, symbol of the Cohens (priests), and a jug and

basin, symbol of the Levis (who, according to tradition, washed the hands of the Cohens).

Opposite page: a further view of the Ancient Cemetery.

Pages 94 and 95: column trunks complete with capitals of the Cividal family.

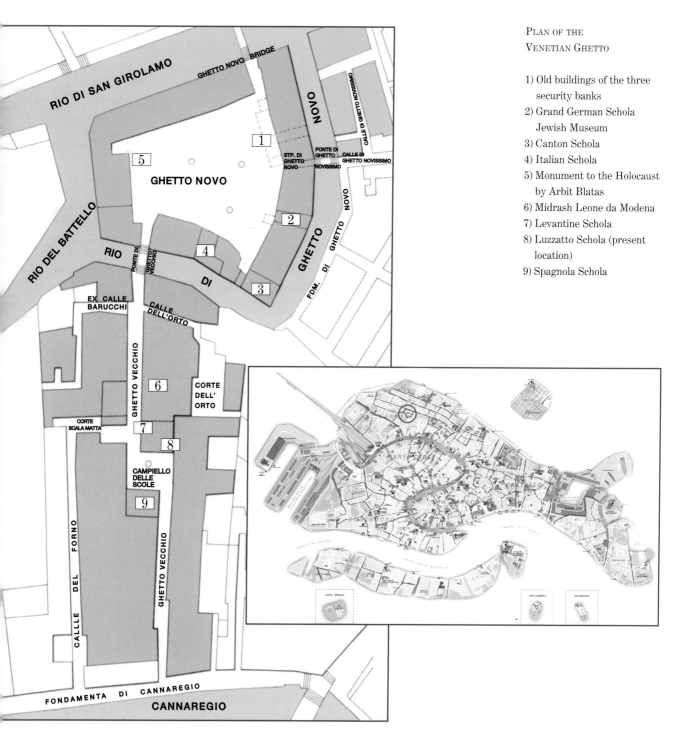

PLAN OF THE
VENETIAN GHETTO

1) Old buildings of the three
   security banks
2) Grand German Schola
   Jewish Museum
3) Canton Schola
4) Italian Schola
5) Monument to the Holocaust
   by Arbit Blatas
6) Midrash Leone da Modena
7) Levantine Schola
8) Luzzatto Schola (present
   location)
9) Spagnola Schola

Art Director
Dario Tagliabue

Layout
Giorgio Gardel

Editorial Coordinator
Caterina Giavotto

Editing
Gail Swerling

Technical Coordinator
Mario Farè

Quality Control
Giancarlo Berti

Translation
Globe Srl Foligno

Photograph Credits
Mondadori Electa Archive, Milan
Davide Calimani, Venice

www.electaweb.com

Reprint 2008

© 2005 by Mondadori Electa S.p.A., Milan
All rights reserved

Printing completed in June 2008
at Artes Gráficas di Toledo, S.A.
Printed in Spain